MELODIC**ROCK**
SOLOING**FOR**GUITAR

Master the Art of Creative, Musical Lead Guitar Playing

SIMON**PRATT**

FUNDAMENTAL**CHANGES**

Melodic Rock Soloing For Guitar

Master the Art of Creative, Musical Lead Guitar Playing

ISBN: 978-1-910403-36-5

Published by **www.fundamental-changes.com**

www.fundamental-changes.com

Over 11,000 fans on Facebook: **FundamentalChangesInGuitar**

Instagram: **FundamentalChanges**

For over 350 Free Guitar Lessons With Videos Check Out

www.fundamental-changes.com

A special thanks to Nick Pratt, Viv Pratt and Jason Sidwell for your hard work and contributions to this book.

Cover Image © Shutterstock: Billion Photos

Contents

Introduction

Ever since Blues guitar players cranked up their small valve amps to create overdriven tones, rock guitar playing has been a dominant force in music. Combining Blues phrasing, melodic licks and modern technical playing, it is no surprise that rock has become so popular. "Rock and Roll" developed in the 1950s and was heavily influenced by The Blues, Country, and R&B styles. By the early 1960s, many sub-genres were appearing, and bands like The Beatles and The Animals led the way in the "British Invasion". The Blues-Rock genre emerged via bands like the Rolling Stones and the Yardbirds, and 'Psychedelic' rock also became popular.

Although Blues-Rock guitarists such as Eric Clapton, Jimmy Page and Jeff Beck pushed the boundaries of what was possible on the electric guitar, no one had more impact on rock music in the '60s than *Mr James Marshall Hendrix*. Jimi Hendrix's unique blend of Blues, Rock, R&B and Psychedelia continues to sound fresh and exciting to this day, despite his recordings being over forty years old. In just three years, from 1967-1970, Hendrix changed how the world perceived the electric guitar, and many regard him as the king of rock guitar.

If Hendrix opened the door for the electric guitar to become more technical and outlandish, Eddie Van Halen redefined the genre in the late '70s. The rock guitar world was speechless when they saw the use of the picking hand 'tapping' notes on the fretboard in conjunction with normal fretted notes. Van Halen cleared the path for the shred heroes of the '80s, such as Joe Satriani, Steve Vai and Yngwie Malmsteen, who built on Van Halen's revolutionary technique and focused on speed, technique and virtuosity.

This book teaches the techniques and skills that will take your melodic rock guitar soloing to a new level. We will look at the core techniques needed to create your own melodic rock guitar licks, and how to phrase your lines beautifully. There is even a whole chapter about how to build a complete solo from a simple melody.

The audio for this book is available from **http://www.fundamental-changes.com/download-audio** so that you can hear how I play and *phrase* each example. The backing tracks provide a perfect platform for you to explore each lick and technique featured in this book.

To give some insight about how the rock guitar genre has evolved, the diagram on the next page shows the most influential and genre-defining rock guitarists. As well as working through all the examples presented in this book, it is crucial to build a catalogue of albums by these artists to expand your melodic rock horizons. Be sure to check out the discography at the end of the book for essential albums by these prolific players.

All the examples in this book are designed to inspire your creativity, but the most fundamental principle is to enjoy yourself and have fun playing music.

Happy Playing!

Simon

Simple Rock Guitar Tree

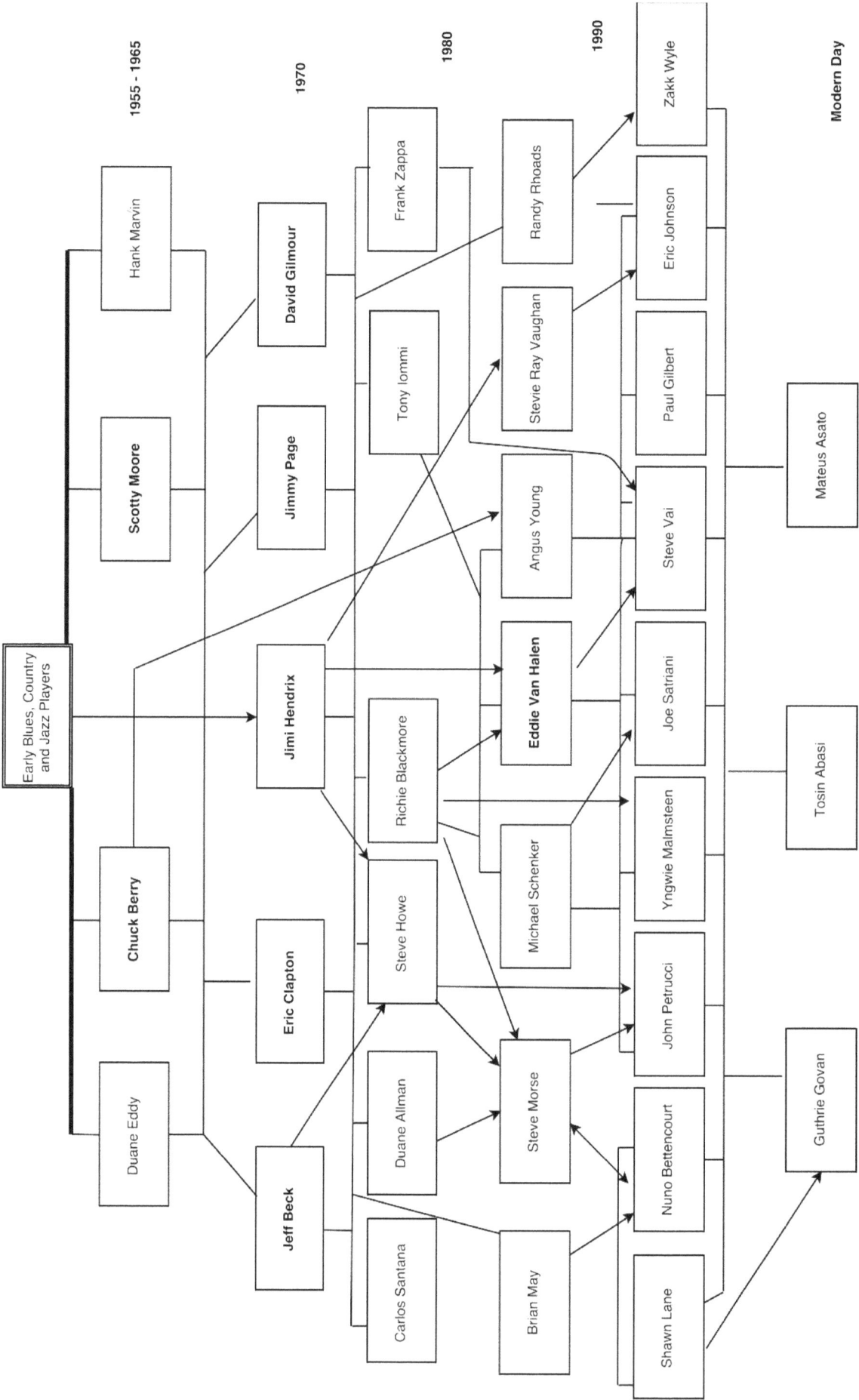

Early Blues, Country and Jazz Players

1955 - 1965

Hank Marvin

Scotty Moore

Chuck Berry

Duane Eddy

1970

David Gilmour

Jimmy Page

Jimi Hendrix

Eric Clapton

Jeff Beck

Frank Zappa

Tony Iommi

Richie Blackmore

Steve Howe

Duane Allman

Carlos Santana

1980

Randy Rhoads

Stevie Ray Vaughan

Angus Young

Eddie Van Halen

Michael Schenker

Steve Morse

Brian May

1990

Zakk Wyle

Eric Johnson

Paul Gilbert

Steve Vai

Joe Satriani

Yngwie Malmsteen

John Petrucci

Nuno Bettencourt

Shawn Lane

Modern Day

Mateus Asato

Tosin Abasi

Guthrie Govan

Get the Audio

The audio files for this book are available to download for free from www.fundamental-changes.com. The link is in the top right-hand corner. Simply select this book title from the drop-down menu and follow the instructions to get the audio.

We recommend that you download the files directly to your computer, not to your tablet, and extract them there before adding them to your media library. You can then put them on your tablet, iPod or burn them to CD. On the download page there is a help PDF and we also provide technical support via the contact form.

For over 350 Free Lessons with Videos Check out:

www.fundamental-changes.com

Over 11,000 fans on Facebook: **FundamentalChangesInGuitar**

Instagram: **FundamentalChanges**

Chapter One – Core Soloing Techniques

There are five main fretting-hand techniques used when playing lead guitar: slides, bends, hammer-ons, pull-offs and vibrato. These five techniques form the basis of almost every melody or solo you play. This chapter breaks down these five techniques and shows you how to use them in a fluid, musical way. Think of this chapter as going to the guitar gym to build strength and coordination for later.

Follow along with the corresponding audio tracks to hear how each technique is broken down into small pieces.

Slides

Backing Track One

The concept of a slide is simple: Fret a note on any string, pick it, and then slide your finger to another note on the same string without re-picking. There are only two types of slides, an upward slide (from a lower pitch to a higher one), and a downward slide (from a higher pitch to a lower one).

The following examples are based around the A Minor Pentatonic scale (A C D E G).

A Minor Pentatonic (Position one).

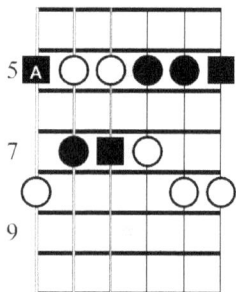

Use your first finger to play Example 1a.

Example 1a (Slide from the 5th to 7th fret on the D string)

You may have found that after you picked the first pitch, the note died as you tried to slide it up to the 7th fret. The crucial thing when sliding is to apply continuous pressure to the string to keep the note ringing.

Repeat Example 1a but apply consistent pressure to the note as you slide it upwards.

Example 1b is identical to 1a, except that you will repeat each slide four times using each finger once. It is important to ensure you are comfortable applying slides on different fingers, so that when you are improvising you won't have to worry about which finger to use.

Keep practicing Example 1b until the slide sounds fluid and effortless on all four fingers.

Example 1b (Slide from the 5th to 7th fret with each finger)

Example 1c introduces a *double slide*. This time, slide from the 5th fret to the 7th fret and back to the 5th fret all with one pick stroke. Once again, it is crucial to keep the pressure on the string while sliding. Aim to slide into the middle of the fret to avoid unwanted buzzes and muting.

Example 1c (Slide from 5th to 7th to 5th on the D string)

The next exercise repeats Example 1c, but now uses all four fingers to help build dexterity and coordination. Start off slowly with a metronome or backing track to keep you in time. Aim to reach 80bpm (beats per minute) while playing two notes per click then gradually increase the speed to reach 100bpm and beyond.

Example 1d (Slide from 5th to 7th to 5th all fingers)

When sliding notes on the guitar, push down only as hard as you need to in order to keep the note ringing. Excessively heavy fretting will make the sliding movement less fluid. Focus your eyes on the fret you are aiming for so that your fingers have a clear target.

Moving Beyond the Basics

So far, we have looked at how to create a slide and how to get it to sound smooth on all four fingers. These slides have been played over short distances, but we can slide any distance on the guitar.

Example 1e shows the A Minor Pentatonic scale played on the D string and demonstrates how to slide between each note to create a fun, rocky melody. On the audio track, I use my first finger, but you should try each finger individually to develop strength and control.

Example 1e (A Minor Pentatonic on the D string)

A Minor Pentatonic (D String Only)

Example 1f is similar to Example 1e but descends the scale from the high A note at the 19th fret. Play this lick on different finger sets to work on your dexterity.

Example 1f (A Minor Pentatonic on the D string reversed)

By combining examples 2e and 2f, we create a longer, four-bar melodic rock line perfectly suited to the A Minor backing track.

Example 1g

One useful application of slides is to move between different scale shapes on the guitar. Sliding up or down from one position to the next creates a fluid sound that is wonderful for melodic guitar playing.

The next example moves between positions one and two of the A Minor Pentatonic scale (shown below) to create a Blues-Rock lick in the key of A minor.

Example 1h

A Minor Pentatonic
Position 1 / E Shape

A Minor Pentatonic
Position 2 / D Shape

Example 1i seamlessly slides between positions three and four of the A Minor Pentatonic scale. These mini licks act as fantastic starting points for your own improvised solos. Slide-based licks always sound melodic and work well as the central theme of a melodic rock solo.

Example 1i

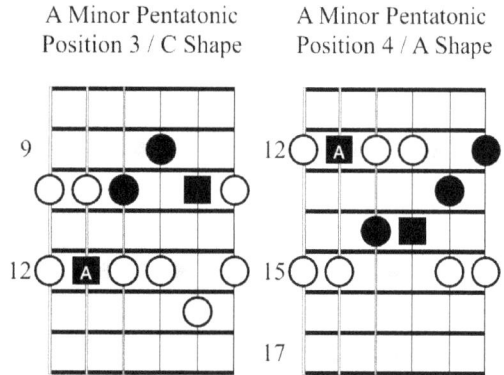

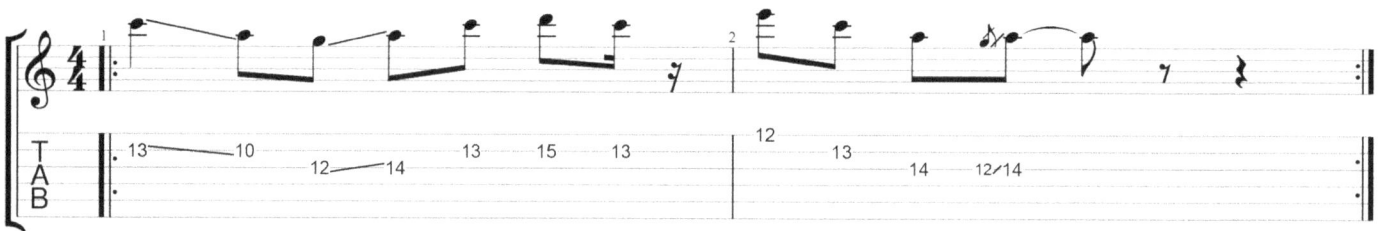

Example 1j uses slides to move between positions one and five of the A Minor Pentatonic scale. Try connecting any two A Minor Pentatonic scale positions together on a single string using your new sliding skills

Play the A Minor backing track and combine examples 2h, 2i and 2j to form a longer melodic idea.

Example 1j

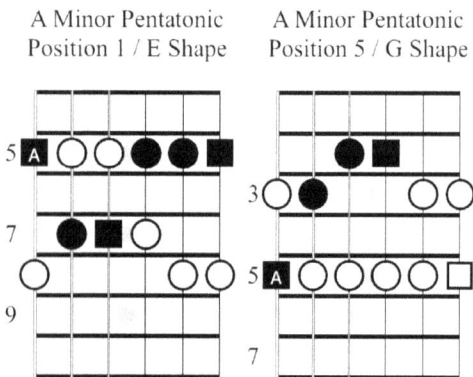

Example 1k uses all five positions of the A Minor Pentatonic scale, but only on the top B and the E strings. By using an anchor note on the B string, and sliding between each position on the high E string, this example demonstrates the ease of moving between scale positions with slides.

The neck diagram below shows the notes of the A Minor Pentatonic scale on the top two strings.

Example 1k

A Minor Pentatonic - Top 2 Strings

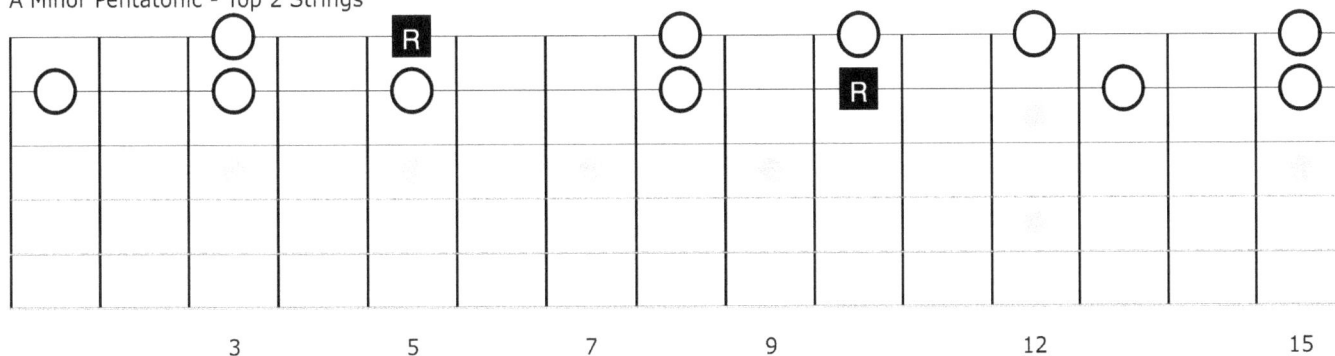

The next lick demonstrates a similar principle to Example 1k, but starts high up the neck and descends through the scale. Using the neck diagram shown above you can experiment with both ascending and descending ideas using slides.

Example 1l

This principle works for any two-string group, and Example 1m demonstrates a similar idea on the G and the B strings. As with all the other examples featured, use the licks provided over the A minor backing track and combine them with your own improvised ideas as well. This will help to *internalise* the musical idea and make it part of your own personal expression.

Example 1m

A Minor Pentatonic - G and B Strings

Example 1n adds *string-skips* to a sliding pattern on the A, G, and high E strings. This type of lick is helpful when learning to break out of traditional 'box' scale shapes because it easily incorporates much of the fretboard.

Shown below is the A Minor Pentatonic scale on the A G and high E strings only. This diagram makes it clear to see how the sliding lick was created. Be careful when you learn this, you may need to use different fingerings to how you previously fretted the scales.

A Minor Pentatonic - A, G, E Strings Only

Example 1n

In a similar fashion to Example 1n, Example 1o uses string-skipped slides, but they are now played on the E, D, and B strings. Solo just with string-skipped slides over a backing track and you will find that the whole fretboard opens up to an incredible amount of new ideas.

Example 1o

A Minor Pentatonic - E, D, B Strings Only

Chapter Two – String Bending

Bending is the technique of raising the pitch of a note by increasing the tension on the string. String bending produces a smooth, expressive sound and gives a 'vocal' quality to your solos. By bending a string, you can create one, or several new pitches, without picking any other notes. Many famous melodic rock guitarists including David Gilmour, Jimi Hendrix and Carlos Santana are all instantly recognisable by their unique approach to string bending.

The idea of a bend is normally to raise the pitch of a fretted note by a set amount. For example, you may wish to bend the string up by a tone (whole-step), or up by a semitone (half-step). Making sure the bend is accurate and in tune is the priority when learning to bend strings. Developing both the strength needed to bend the string and the aural skill to hear when the bent note is in tune requires dedicated practice. The following examples will teach how to bend perfectly in tune.

Consider your string gauge before attempting the exercises in this chapter. It is more difficult to bend thicker (heavier) gauge strings, despite the improved tone they produce. The audio examples were recorded using Ernie Ball Super Slinkys (gauge 9-42).

Types of Bends and Bending in Tune

The whole-tone bend (two-frets) is the most common bend in modern electric guitar playing.

In Example 2a we play the 9th fret of the G string as a reference or 'target' note before bending the 7th fret of the same string upwards until we have replicated the original 9th fret pitch.

Play the 7th fret note with your third finger and place fingers one and two on the same string (behind the fretting finger) to provide strength and support. Always support any bend with spare fingers whenever possible.

Example 2a – (Tone bend)

The semitone (one-fret) bend is another common bend, especially in Blues and Rock guitar. In the next example, the 8th fret of the G string acts as the target pitch when bending up from the 7th fret. This bend requires less force than the previous example.

Example 2b – (Semitone bend)

Although slightly less common than the previous two examples, the tone-and-a-half (three-frets) bend is a useful addition to your vocabulary. This bend requires more force than the previous two examples but is worth the effort. Use the 10th fret of the G string as your reference pitch and then bend the 7th fret until you reach the same pitch.

Example 2c – (Tone-and-a-half-bend)

If you struggle to master Example 2c, stick to examples 2a and 2b until you build up more strength in your fingers.

Example 2d shows a two-tone (four-frets) bend of which David Gilmour a big fan. This example uses the 11th fret of the G string as the reference pitch for the 7th fret bend.

Example 2d – (Two-tone Bend)

There is also a type of tiny bend known as a 'curl.' A 'curl' is the smallest audible distance you can bend a string on the guitar. John Mayer's version of the classic Blues anthem, Crossroads on the album Battle Studies is a bending master-class. He uses curls to significant effect in the solo and demonstrates many subtle nuances of string bending.

Example 2e – (Blues 'curl')

Bending Licks

Now that we have covered the fundamental principles of bending in tune, it is time to introduce some bending vocabulary. The following examples use the A Minor Pentatonic and the A Blues Scales.

This first Blues lick uses shape one of the A Minor Pentatonic scale. The lick demonstrates the whole-tone bend seen in example 2a but adds a few Minor Pentatonic notes to create a classic Blues idea.

Example 2f

Example 2g is a simple A Minor Pentatonic that contains just two notes. You may find some unwanted string noise occurs when changing strings after the bend. Try to place the palm of the picking hand (in a karate chop position) slightly onto the strings by the bridge of the guitar. This will mute the lower strings while the underside of the fretting hand fingers naturally mutes the high E string.

Example 2g

The next example builds on Example 2g to create a longer Pentatonic lick.

Example 2h

Once you are comfortable with bending, you can combine these ideas with the licks in the previous chapter. As you progress, keep soloing over the A minor backing track to create a fun, musical application of everything you learn.

Example 2i is a 'must know' lick, used by almost every classic rock guitarist from Chuck Berry to Angus Young. Roll your first finger through the 5th fret notes, so they sound individually and not together.

Example 2i

The next example builds on the previous idea but incorporates a few more notes from the A Minor Pentatonic scale. Ensure you *roll* your first finger through the 5th fret notes to avoid them playing at the same time.

Example 2j

The next example uses the 8th and the 5th frets of the high E string.

Example 2k

Early rock guitar pioneers like Chuck Berry and Scotty Moore often added *double-stops* (two notes played simultaneously) to bending licks. Example 2l is a classic country-Blues lick in the style of Chuck Berry.

Example 2l

The following is another double-stop rock lick, this time in the style of Angus Young. In this example support the third-finger bend with your second finger and use your first finger to play the notes on the top two strings as a mini-barre.

Example 2m

Example 2n introduces multiple bends within a one bar lick. Begin playing this lick very slowly and aim for clarity and accuracy on each note.

Example 2n

Example 2o builds on Example 2n and incorporates a new note (Eb) from the A Blues Scale.

Example 2o

A Blues
Position 1 / E Shape

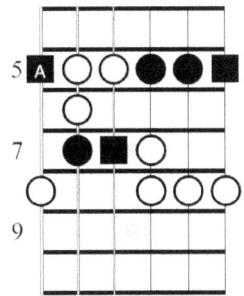

The next example uses the A Minor Pentatonic scale and includes whole-tone bends and a Blues curl.

Example 2p

The following examples show bends in different positions of the A Blues Scale using CAGED shapes. For an explanation of the CAGED system, refer to Appendix One and check out **The CAGED System and 100 Licks for Blues Guitar** by Joseph Alexander.

Example 2q demonstrates the A Blues Scale in position two to create a classic Blues-Rock lick.

As you improve and begin to master each lick, add in any extra melodic techniques you wish, to make each line a part of your own unique musical voice.

Example 2q

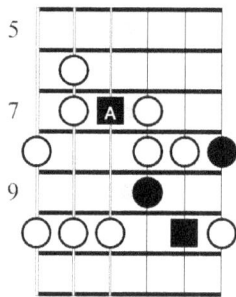

The next example uses position three of the A Blues Scale to create a Blues lick in the style of Albert King. The chromatic run at the beginning gives this lick its character. By repeating an idea and including subtle variations you can easily turn a short lick into a longer phrase.

Example 2r

A Blues
Position 3 / C Shape

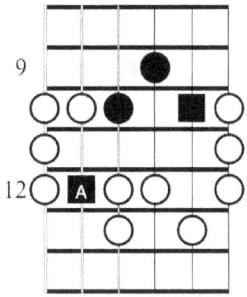

Example 2s shows the A Blues Scale in position four and uses a *call and response* phrase. The rhythm used here is common among Blues and rock licks so include it in your own solos.

Example 2s

A Blues
Position 4 / A Shape

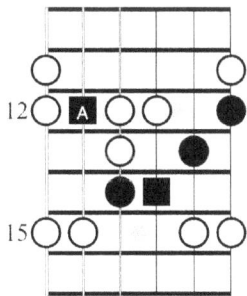

The final example employs alternate picking to create a fast Blues Scale run in position five. Practice this lick at a very slow tempo (around 70bpm), and only speed up when the lick is accurate and clear.

Example 2t

A Blues
Position 5 / G Shape

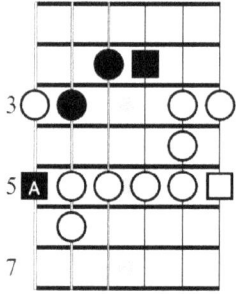

Chapter Three – Legato

In the late 1960s and early 1970s, rock guitarists like Jimmy Page and Brian May began to incorporate faster phrases into their solos. These quicker passages were often created by playing *hammer-ons* and *pull-offs*. Together, these two techniques are referred to as *legato* (Italian for 'smooth') techniques. Some classic examples of legato playing are in Led Zeppelin's Stairway to Heaven solo, Queen's I Want It All solo, and the Red Hot Chili Peppers' track Snow.

To create a hammer-on, play a note and then quickly 'hammer' a different finger onto a higher fret. The result is two notes from just one pick stroke. A pull-off is the reverse of a hammer-on. Begin by picking a fretted note and then pull your finger off the string (downwards towards the floor) to sound a fretted note below the first.

Legato guitar playing is all about smooth, flowing lines, and lends itself perfectly to melodic rock soloing. An important concern when playing legato is to *keep each note the same volume*. This means that the picked note and the legato notes that follow should all have very similar dynamics. Try recording yourself playing the following examples and pay attention to how smooth the transition is between the picked and legato notes.

There are many legato technique-building exercises, and, while useful for developing the fundamental principles, they are often not very musical. The following examples aim to keep every exercise musical while developing great technique. Listen to the audio examples first to hear how these examples should sound before trying them yourself.

Stick to the *one-finger-per-fret* rule when learning these examples unless otherwise stated. The idea behind the rule is that you allocate one finger to each fret that you play. For example, if you are playing notes between the 5th and 8th frets, use your first finger for the 5th frets notes and your second finger for all 6th frets notes, etc. This can be seen in the diagram below:

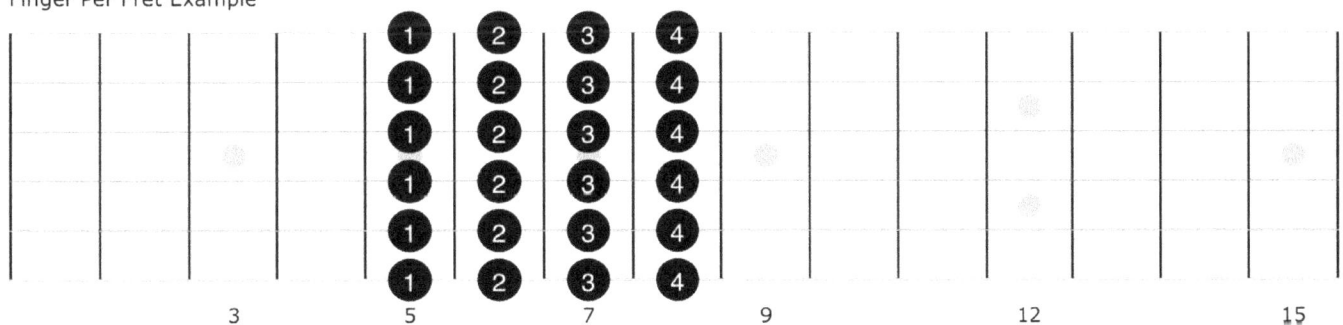

Finger Per Fret Example

Key points to consider:

1) Ensure there is space between the fingers of your fretting hand when playing legato. By learning to play legato with room between your fingers, you will develop strength in the correct tendons and muscles of the hand.

2) Keep your knuckles upright at all times.

3) Stop if you feel any pain. When it comes to guitar playing, 'no pain, no gain' is *never* the way forward. Stretch and warm up thoroughly before you play difficult legato sequences and stop if you feel any strain.

The simplest legato technique is the semitone (one-fret) hammer-on which is demonstrated in the first example. Use your first and second fingers to play this exercise and keep some space between your fingers to help build strength and good technique.

Example 3a – (One fret / semitone hammer-on)

On paper, Example 3b looks identical to example 3a but it is played differently.

In Example 3a we used our two strongest fingers to complete the one fret hammer-on. In Example 3b, we cycle through all the finger combinations that may occur. Start with fingers one and two, then two and three, then three and four before returning to fingers two and three. Pay attention to the fingering marked on the notation.

This technique-building exercise develops all your fingers at equal rates which is important when building longer, more complex legato patterns.

Example 3b – (One fret semitone hammer-on all fingers)

When playing Blues guitar, it is common to use the Minor Pentatonic scale and add a *major 3rd* when playing over a dominant 7th chord (such as B7).

Example 3c is a simple, Eric Clapton-style B7 lick that uses the one-fret hammer-on learnt earlier.

The diagrams below show a B7 chord and a B Minor Pentatonic scale with the major 3rd included. The diamond blocks show the major 3rd (D#) that is added to create a Bluesy sound. Remember that a solid foundation in Blues vocabulary is essential when building melodic rock soloing ideas.

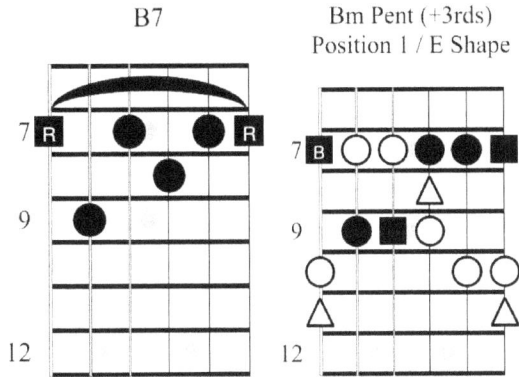

Example 3c – ('Clapton-style' Blues lick using one-fret hammer-on)

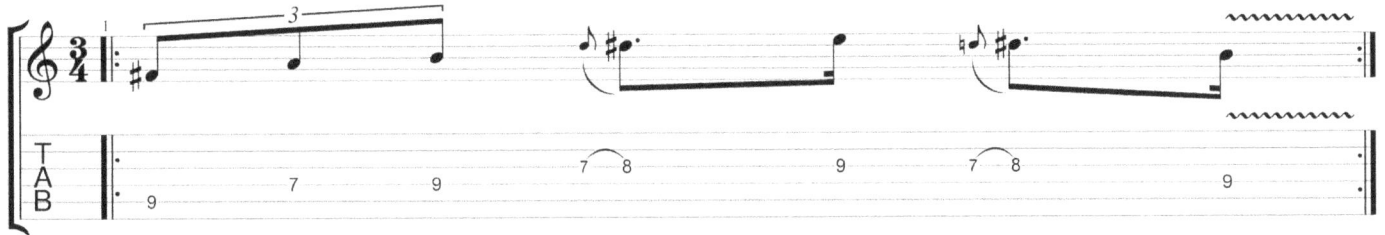

Example 3d applies the same notes and rhythms to position two.

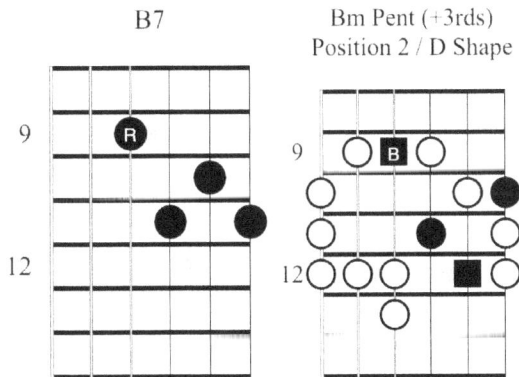

Example 3d – ('Clapton-style' shape two lick)

The next example demonstrates a two-fret (whole-tone) hammer-on using the first and third fingers of the fretting hand. The whole-tone hammer-on is common, so it is important to become extremely familiar with it. Ensure the knuckle of the 3rd finger stays upright when playing this example.

Example 3e – (Two-fret whole-tone hammer-on)

It is possible to play three different two-fret hammer-ons in the first position of the Minor Pentatonic scale. In Example 3f, I have combined all three into a popular Blues-Rock lick that works well over a Bm chord or progression.

Example 3f – (B Minor Pentatonic lick with two-fret hammer-on)

The next example is a chord sequence of Bm, Asus2 and G. To start and finish the chord sequence, I play a simple legato run using a two-note hammer-on in B Minor Pentatonic position four. The addition of a scale run to a chord sequence blends rhythm and lead guitar together into an interesting texture.

Example 3g – (B Minor chord sequence using two-fret hammer-ons)

B Minor Pentatonic
Position 4 / A Shape

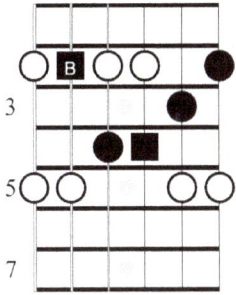

Example 3h introduces a three-fret hammer-on. The fourth finger usually needs more training than the others, so push the finger into the fretboard firmly to create the same volume as the pick stroke that preceded it.

Example 3h – (Three-fret hammer-on)

The following example is a Blues-Rock lick in the style of players like Eric Johnson and Joe Bonamassa. If you are struggling to play this lick using your 4th finger, try using your 3rd finger instead.

Example 3i – (B Minor Pentatonic lick with three-fret hammer-ons)

The final example introduces the four-fret hammer-on. Although it is possible to hammer-on further than four frets, it is a rarely needed skill.

Example 3j – (Four-fret hammer-on)

Chapter Four – Vibrato

I believe that vibrato is the most important technique for any guitarist to master and I can always tell a student's ability simply by the confidence they have when they apply vibrato. Often, we spend so much time trying to develop speed and other techniques that vibrato gets lost in a sea of other distractions. Don't let that be the case! I have deliberately put this chapter early on in this book so you can apply vibrato to all the licks that follow.

Vibrato adds expression to a note by rapidly moving the pitch up and down. This allows a note to have a more vocal, human quality and gives passion and emotion to your melodic rock guitar solos. Vibrato is incredibly unique to each guitarist and can be added to any note with any finger. The amount of vibrato used depends on the genre of music and it is possible to alter its speed, duration, and the delay before it is added after the note is played.

There are two main types of vibrato: 'classical' and 'modern rock'. This chapter focuses primarily on the modern rock technique, although the classical vibrato technique seen below can sound subtle and work beautifully on the acoustic guitar.

'Classical' Vibrato

The difference between classical and modern rock vibrato is the *direction* of movement by which the vibrato is created. Classical vibrato mainly used by nylon-string guitarists is applied *along* the string by stretching the string horizontally with the finger. The speed at which the finger is moved from side to side dictates the amount of vibrato added to the note.

As well as the ideas shown here, try adding delicate classical vibrato to licks you already know and sync the speed of the vibrato to the track you are playing.

Developing good technique on all fingers will allow you to add vibrato to any note whenever you feel it appropriate. This first exercise uses chromatic notes between the 7th and 10th frets on the G string. Bar one ends with your first finger, bar two with your second, bar three with your third and bar four with your fourth. Pay close attention to the fingering shown in the notation.

Example 4a – (Classical vibrato on all fingers)

The next example is a melody created from the C Natural Minor scale (C D Eb F G Ab Bb) and incorporates some subtle classical vibrato. Make the vibrato delicate so that it enhances the sound without becoming a distraction.

Example 4b – (Simple melody with classical-style vibrato)

Example 4c shows a double-stop pattern in the key of E minor that uses classical vibrato to punctuate the musical phrase.

Example 4c – (Double-stops with classical vibrato)

When we improvise, we often concentrate on single note melodies, but adding double-stops can inject new fresh creative ideas into our lead playing. Shown below are the notes of the E Natural Minor scale on the D and the B strings.

E Natural Minor - 'D' and 'B' Strings

Although it is possible to create double-stop patterns anywhere on the neck, in a lead playing context using the thinner, high pitched strings is preferred. Shown below is the E Natural Minor scale (E F# G A B C D) on the G and the E strings. These double-stops sound fantastic and work well with the classical vibrato technique described above.

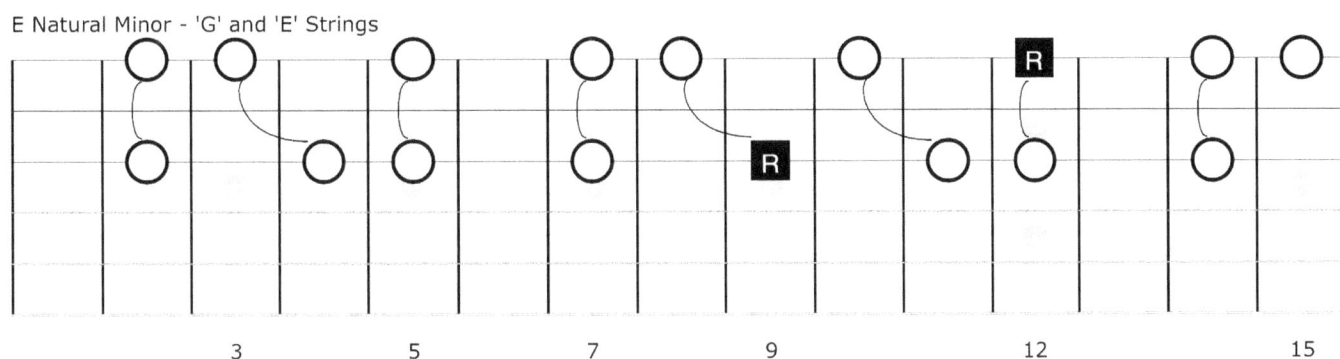

E Natural Minor - 'G' and 'E' Strings

Use the previous two neck diagrams to explore soloing with double-stops in the key of E minor.

Modern Rock Vibrato

Modern rock vibrato is applied in the direction of the fret wire in a similar way to bending a string. This technique gives greater control of the pitch variation of a note, and also allows us to add vibrato to a bend. Soft, gentle vibrato suits ballads and slower songs, while wide vibrato (manipulating the string further) works well for harder rock tracks.

Example 4d – (Basic Modern Rock Vibrato Technique)

1. Pick and hold the 7th fret of the G string with your first finger.

2. Place your thumb slightly over the neck, as if you were going to bend the note.

3. Pull the string down towards the floor using your wrist as a pivot. The vibrato is created by the manipulation of the wrist, rather than the fingers. Release the wrist back to a normal position and let the note return to its original pitch.

4. Repeat this movement as many times as possible, although three times is usually enough in practice.

5. Repeat Example 4d on each finger. (The fourth finger is used less often, but it is still good practice if you can manage it).

At first, the string might not move very far, but, just as with string bending, it becomes much easier with practice.

When you are comfortable with this basic approach, experiment with the amount of vibrato you add and the speed of the manipulation.

The most crucial thing when applying modern rock vibrato is to ensure that the note doesn't sound out of tune when the vibrato is applied. The more confident you become at using vibrato, the wider the vibrato you can add.

Classical vibrato and modern rock vibrato are distinguished in the notation by the size of the vibrato lines above the notes. Classical vibrato has a thin line, and rock vibrato has a much thicker line.

Years ago, I watched Steve Vai warming up before a show. He practiced vibrato before he went on stage and showed me a brilliant warm-up exercise that I still use to this day. He started with his first finger on the 3rd fret of the G string and added vibrato to that note. He then slid up an octave to the 15th fret and applied vibrato to that note too. He then repeated the technique using his *second finger* on the 4th and 16th frets, adding vibrato to both before repeating the process for each finger. This exercise is shown in Example 4e.

Steve Vai's vibrato warm-up develops all four fingers of your fretting hand and gets you used to adding vibrato in different parts of the neck. It is normally far easier to add vibrato higher up the fretboard.

Example 4e – (Steve Vai octave vibrato)

Another good vibrato exercise is 'random note' vibrato. Pick any note on the guitar and add vibrato to it with whatever finger you land on. This technique breaks you out of the habit of only adding vibrato with certain fingers.

In Example 4f, I have placed a few notes around the fretboard for you to add vibrato to. Don't worry if this example doesn't sound musical, it is not supposed to; it is just a good technique builder.

Example 4f – (Random note vibrato)

Conclusion

Mimicry is an excellent way to work on vibrato. Listen to your favourite artists and identify what it is about their sound that excites you, because this will help you to craft your own unique sound. Listen to David Gilmour (Pink Floyd), Steve Lukather (Toto), Gary Moore, and Paul Gilbert to hear their unique and individual approaches to vibrato.

As you progress through the rest of this book, pay special attention to the vibrato in each example. Listen carefully to how I play each lick, and hear just how much difference vibrato can make. Even the simplest lick can be transformed into an emotive, expressive idea!

Chapter Five – Advanced Bending Techniques

In this chapter, we will explore some more advanced approaches that will help you to get the most out of your bending ideas. Jeff Beck is a master of bending, so before working through this chapter listen to his version of Goodbye Pork Pie Hat to prepare your ears sonically for the licks to come.

The Pre-Bend

A Pre-bend is the technique of bending the string up to the required pitch *before* picking the note. This is tricky to achieve as you have to learn how far to bend the string without being able to hear if it is correct.

In the last chapter, we practiced bends by using our ears to ensure each bend was perfectly in tune. With pre-bends, we don't have the option to use our ears as our guide and must rely on the technique of the bend to be accurate.

Example 5a – (Whole-tone pre-bend)

Example 5b demonstrates the same technique using a semitone (one-fret) bend instead of a whole tone, (two-fret) bend.

Example 5b – (Semitone pre-bend)

The next example shows a tone-and-a-half (three-fret) pre-bend. The bigger the pre-bend, the harder it is to pitch accurately and keep in tune.

Example 5c – (Tone-and-a-half Pre-Bend)

The two-tone pre-bend is difficult due to its size. Don't attempt this example until you are comfortable with examples 5a, 5b and 5c. To achieve bends of this size, it helps to use lighter string gauges. Jimmy Page uses 8-42 gauge strings giving him the ability to play the enormous bends heard on tracks like Stairway To Heaven.

Example 5d – (Two-Tone Pre-bend)

Pre-bend and Release

Now that pre-bends feel comfortable and familiar, it is time to use them in context. The most common way to use pre-bends is the *pre-bend and release* technique. By pre-bending a note and then releasing it down to its original pitch, you create a wonderful, emotive wail that is often overlooked in modern-day playing.

The four examples given below show how to apply this technique to examples 5a - 5d.

Example 5e – (Semitone pre-bend/release)

The next example demonstrates a *semitone* pre-bend with release back to the original fretted note of D. Be sure to incorporate these examples immediately into your improvised solos.

Example 5f – (Whole-tone pre-bend/release)

Example 5g uses the tone-and-a-half pre-bend from Example 5c but once again adds the release back to the original fretted note of D. The larger the pre-bend / release, the bigger the 'crying' tone you will create.

Example 5g – (Tone-and-a-half pre-bend/release)

David Gilmour is a huge fan of the *two-tone* bend and it is often referred to as the 'Gilmour Bend'. It isn't easy to achieve a two-tone pre-bend and release, so take your time and follow along with the audio track.

Example 5h – (Two-tone pre-bend/release)

Pre-bend Licks

Example 5i is an A Minor Pentatonic lick that uses a whole-tone pre-bend at the 7th fret of the G string. This pre-bend is commonly used in Rock and Blues solos, so take your time to master the exact technique shown here.

Example 5i – (A Minor Pentatonic pre-bend lick)

By keeping licks bite-sized, they are easier to learn and implement into your solos.

The next example builds on the phrase above and creates a longer line that uses both pre-, and normal bends. The true art in bending is being able to blend all the different types of bends together. So, after you have worked through each lick, be sure to include it in your improvisation as quickly as possible.

Example 5j – (Extended A Minor Pentatonic pre-bend lick)

Example 5k uses multiple pre-bends and moves up trough the A Minor Pentatonic scale to create a David Gilmour-style melodic rock lick. This idea demonstrates a useful way to move between different scale patterns on the guitar. By building a phrase on just one string, you can create long, fluid licks between scale shapes you are familiar with.

Example 5k – (Multiple pre-bends)

The next idea uses positions four and one of the A Minor Pentatonic scale and incorporates multiple pre-bends to create my favourite lick of this chapter. This lick uses a classic rock technique of jumping between positions before resolving to the root note (A) at the end of bar two.

Example 5l

We have studied bends in different positions of the A Minor Pentatonic scale, but Example 5m uses the A *Major Pentatonic* scale and incorporates pre-bends to create a happier sounding lick. Slash often used the Major Pentatonic scale to create his memorable solos on Guns N' Roses tracks like Paradise City.

Example 5m – (A Major Pentatonic with pre-bends)

Example 5n concludes our look at pre-bends and uses position three of the A Major Pentatonic scale to create an effective lick that fits perfectly over an A Major chord sequence.

Example 5n – (A Major Pentatonic scale position three with pre-bends)

A Major Pentatonic
Position 3 / C Shape

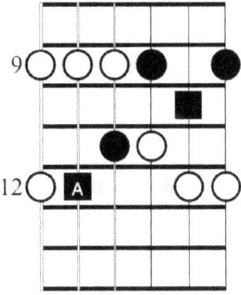

The Square Bend

Now that the basics of bending in tune have been covered, we can explore some ways to create different effects. There are two main types of bend, the square bend and the circular bend. These terms refer to how the bend is created. The square bend is a harsh bend that is quickly executed and released. This technique is very common among modern Rock/Metal guitarists as well as Country guitarists who wish to emulate the pedal steel guitar's 'mechanised' string bending sound. Listen carefully to the audio track before playing the next example, as simply reading the notation doesn't show the underlying subtlety of the bend.

Example 5o – (Square bends with A Minor Pentatonic)

The Circular Bend

The circular bend is a smoother (and/or slower) transition from a picked note to a bend. This bend is often heard in Blues and Melodic Rock, and is much more commonly played. Once again, listen to the corresponding audio track, as the tablature and notation cannot accurately show the way the notes are phrased.

Circular Bend / Release

On paper, Example 5p looks identical to Example 5o, and only by listening will you understand the difference between the two approaches. Listen for the smoother bends and transitions in Example 5p compared to Example 5o. You will, of course, wish to use a mixture of bending techniques depending on the solo you are playing.

Example 5p – (Circular bends with A Minor Pentatonic)

When I first started to explore what could be achieved with bending, I was amazed at the versatility of the technique. By just adding pre-bends to your solos, you can replicate some of the delicate phrasing of guitarists like David Gilmour, Eric Clapton and Carlos Santana.

Chapter Six – Advanced Bending Techniques Part Two

This chapter examines some advanced bending techniques that are often used in guitar solos. As with all other chapters in this book, it is essential that you learn to *apply* these techniques as quickly as possible, so use the backing track provided as a basis for your improvisation.

Unison Bends

Musically, when something is said to be in unison, it means that two or more notes are played simultaneously and at the same pitch. On the guitar, it is possible to create a unison via a *unison bend*. Countless players, including Carlos Santana, Van Halen, Jimi Hendrix, and many more have used this technique to great effect!

A unison bend occurs when one note is bent up to sound identical to another note on an adjacent string. This is demonstrated in the following example.

Play the 5th fret of the B string and bend the 7th fret of the G string until it sounds identical to the first note. Getting unison bends perfectly in tune is critical, otherwise the effect will sound terrible! Listen to the audio track to hear how this should sound.

Example 6a – (Basic unison bend)

It is important to use this technique in a musical context as quickly as possible. Example 6b teaches you an A Minor Pentatonic lick that includes a unison bend on the top two strings.

Example 6b – (Minor Pentatonic unison bend lick)

The next example ascends the A Minor Pentatonic scale on the high E string and plays each note of the scale as a unison bend. Carlos Santana uses this type of idea to connect different scale shapes and to add a raw, rocky texture to his Latin licks.

Example 6c – (Minor Pentatonic full-scale unison bends)

Example 6d shows the A Major Pentatonic scale on the high E string and plays each note of the scale as a unison bend.

Example 6d – (Major Pentatonic full-scale unison bends)

The next few examples show unison bends in the style of some influential melodic guitarists. They are played in different keys to keep things interesting and to open up the fretboard for you.

Hendrix was an innovator of many bending techniques, and Example 6f is a unison bend lick in his style. Begin slowly (at around 70 bpm) and gradually increase the tempo when each element is accurate.

Example 6f – (F#m Hendrix-style unison bends)

Andy Summers is a guitarist who is often more revered for his rhythm work than his lead playing. Mixed quietly into tracks like Message in a Bottle by The Police, Summers often added simple, effective lead lines that included unison bends. Example 6g uses the D Natural Minor scale (D E F G A Bb C) to create a simple call and response blues-rock phrase.

Example 6g – (Andy Summers-style unison bend)

D Natural Minor
Position 1 (E Shape)

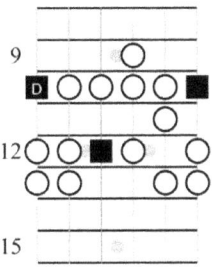

This classic Carlos Santana lick uses unison bends in B Harmonic Minor (B C# D E F# G A#) and has a distinctly Spanish/Latin flavour. Use this lick as a starting point to create solos and explore the scale shape above to add some sophisticated sounds to your minor improvisation.

Example 6h – (Carlos Santana-style unison bend)

B Harmonic Minor
Position 1 (E Shape)

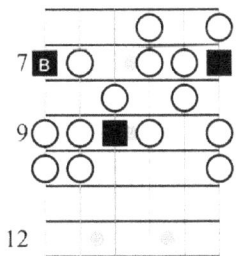

The next example introduces *tremolo-picking* in the style of Eddie Van Halen. Tremolo-picking is the technique of alternate picking each note as fast as possible. Van Halen made this technique famous in the final run of the Michael Jackson Beat It solo. The tremolo-picked line demonstrated here uses the E Natural Minor scale (E F# G A B C D), before adding a unison bend to resolve the lick.

Example 6i – (Van Halen-style unison bend)

As you can see, unison bends provide an exciting addition to your soloing vocabulary and break the mould of traditional patterns and licks. Experimenting with this technique is great fun, but ensure that your bends are perfectly in tune, otherwise you will create some dissonant, wild screeches that are not easy on the ear!

Broken Unison Bends

The last few examples demonstrated how the unison bend can add texture to your solos. Another approach is to break up the notes by picking each one *separately*. The guitar is wonderfully versatile, so even when you think you know everything about a technique like bending, you can always dive deeper and find exciting new sounds.

In Example 6j, we break up unison bends in the key of C Phrygian (C Db Eb F G Ab Bb) to create a modern-sounding melodic rock lead line. Practicing this example is a good way to ensure your unison bends are in tune.

Example 6j – (C Phrygian Broken Unison Bends)

This next lick has hints of David Gilmour throughout. It uses broken unison bends to create the main sound while moving between different positions of the D Minor Pentatonic scale. Any unison bend lick can be made into a broken unison bend by picking the notes separately instead of together, so recap over the examples in this chapter and create broken unison bend licks from them.

Example 6k – (Dm Broken Unison Bends)

Bend Vibrato

Often the simplest phrases sound beautifully crafted when vibrato is added.

Use the wrist-based technique taught in the earlier vibrato chapter, and carefully listen to the audio examples to hear how I apply vibrato throughout the following licks and ideas.

In the first example, bend the 7th fret of the G string as normal, before adding wide Blues-Rock vibrato. Be sure only to add the vibrato after the desired pitch is reached. When applying the vibrato, manipulate the string back and forth, but don't waver too much from the target pitch (E).

Example 6l – (Basic bend vibrato G string)

In the next example, we apply the same technique as in Example 6l, but add vibrato to a bend on the B string at the 8th fret. As with bending, adding vibrato becomes easier the higher up the fretboard that you go.

Example 6m – (Basic bend vibrato B string)

Example 6n is an A Minor Pentatonic lick played on the G string that uses three, back-to-back vibrato bends. Playing multiple bends on one string can be extremely powerful. Adding vibrato to these bends adds a vocal, human quality to the lick.

Example 6n – (Multiple vibrato bends on one string)

Example 6o adds vibrato to a blues theme we played earlier.

Example 6o – (Blues lick with a vibrato bend)

Next, I've created a C Minor Blues lick with delicate phrasing and expression. The bends and vibrato in this idea demonstrate the melodic touch that the greatest guitarists apply to almost every phrase.

Example 6p – (C Minor Blues-Rock lick)

As you can hear, vibrato transforms even the simplest bend into a vocal cry and is a crucial element in creating melodic rock guitar solos.
Once you feel confident with this technique, add bend vibrato to any licks you already know. You don't have to add vibrato to every bend that you play, so try using it sparingly.

Mini Solo Using Bends

I have written a solo in D Minor to consolidate the techniques studies in the previous sections. Refer to the D Natural Minor scale (D E F G A Bb C) diagram below when learning this solo as most of the notes derive from this scale.

This solo references some great melodic guitarists, such as David Gilmour, Jimi Hendrix, and Carlos Santana. Steal a lick from every bar and add it to your own solos.

Example 6q
Backing Track Two

D Natural Minor

Bending Solo in D Minor

This solo demonstrates bending vocabulary in several different ways. There are whole-tone (two-fret) bends, semitone (one-fret) bends and also unison bends. Ensure that your bends are perfectly in tune and add vibrato to punctuate each phrase.

Listen to the albums recommended in the discography for many examples of beautifully constructed solos and transcribe your favourite licks by ear.

Chapter Seven – Hybrid Picking

Hybrid picking is the technique of using the pick and fingers of your picking hand together. The advantage of hybrid picking is that it is far easier to move between strings, especially when crossing multiple strings. You can also cut down the number of pick strokes needed, ultimately leading to a fluid sound. The dynamic variation and timbre of the notes that are struck with the fingers is also a huge plus.

Hybrid picking was popularised by 'progressive' rock guitarists such as Steve Howe in the '80s, but these days the technique has been adopted by many players because of its speed and flexibility. Players like Guthrie Govan and Eric Johnson have pushed technical boundaries and often include hybrid picking in their melodic arsenal.

This chapter helps you to gain confidence with hybrid picking as the technique may feel strange at first. I have included the most common variations used in hybrid picking, such as single-note lines, double-stop licks and simple triad chords. The picking you should use is given in the notation:

'M' means use your second finger to pick the note, and 'A' means use your third finger.

As always, there is no rush to play these licks at lightening speeds. Begin very slowly at around 60/70bpm, and only increase the metronome speed when you can play each lick perfectly five times in a row. If a specific lick feels particularly uncomfortable with the fingering provided, feel free to adapt how you pick it.

The first example shows a basic hybrid-picking pattern using notes of the B Minor Pentatonic scale. This example alternates between using a down-pick on the D string and second-finger pick on the G string.

Make sure that your down-stroke and second finger pick are dynamically even.

Example 7a

In the next example, use the third finger to pick the 7th fret of the B string. The third finger often feels weaker than the second finger when learning to hybrid pick. This is perfectly natural and with dedicated practice it will become as strong and developed as the second finger.

Example 7b

The following example combines examples 7a and 7b to provide an effective warm-up pattern. Learning to alternate between using your pick, second and third finger is the key to developing fluidity in hybrid picking.

Example 7c

Example 7d reverses Example 7c and teaches you how to start a picking pattern with a finger pick.

Example 7d

Hybrid picking lets you pick multiple notes simultaneously. This is especially useful when playing double-stops. Keep your second and third fingers "glued" together when picking this next example.

Example 7e

Example 7f shows the reverse of Example 7e. Play the double-stop with your second and third fingers, before picking the root note with a down-pick.

Example 7f

Moving double-stops between strings can prove tricky, but hybrid picking can simplify the task. Two different B Minor Pentatonic double-stops are demonstrated in the next example and are punctuated by a down-pick on the D string.

Example 7g

Example 7h reverses Example 7g, demonstrating how to create multiple licks from one simple idea.

Example 7h

The triad (three-note chord) shown in Example 7i can be thought of as either a Bm7 chord or a D major chord.

Example 7i

Example 7j uses the triad chord shape in the previous example, but applies a different picking hand pattern. Pay close attention to the picking directions for each example in this chapter.

Example 7j

Example 7k shows another common hybrid picked pattern that uses the triad chord introduced in 7i. By learning these hybrid-picking patterns, you develop the technique needed to write licks, play triad chords, and build solos that utilise hybrid picking.

Example 7k

Example 7l is a chord sequence that is played with hybrid picking. Learn each chord shape first and strum through them before applying the hybrid-picking pattern shown below. This example may look challenging, but the picking hand repeats the same pattern throughout the whole chord sequence.

Example 7l

Example 7m shows a favourite hybrid picking of Eric Johnson. Eric creates lovely chord voicings that utilise adjacent strings and a string skip. Notice here that we have two down-picks followed by a second finger pick throughout. Playing string skips with hybrid picking is easy as each string is within easy reach.

Example 7m

This next chord-based idea uses three-note triads with each note played simultaneously. The chord sequence demonstrated here is a very common funk-rock pattern in the key of E minor.

Example 7n

Example 7o uses the same chord progression as the previous example, but instead of playing all the notes of the triad together it introduces a *call and response* rhythmic pattern. Play all three notes together, then alternate between a down-pick and a double-stop. This may require more practice than some of the previous examples, but it will help you to add melodic-rock chord textures to your solos.

Example 7o

Now we come to some single note 'lick builders'. Example 7p employs hybrid picking and legato to create a very smooth and fluid line.

Example 7p

Lick builder number two uses the principles developed in Example 7p but now introduces a string skip to add melodic interest.

Example 7q

By combining examples 7p and 8q, we can create a new lick. This lick uses legato and alternates between pick strokes, second finger picking, and third finger picking.

Example 7r

Pentatonic scales are a brilliant improvisational tool, especially in melodic rock playing. This example introduces a common, six-note picking pattern. This example will develop the dexterity of your picking hand as you have to focus constantly on which part of the pattern you are playing. Look closely at the picking directions to stop you getting lost.

Example 7s

Once again, use the same framework as the previous example and now create a string skip in the hybrid-picked legato pattern.

Example 7t

Example 7u uses an earlier pattern but moves it through two different areas of the B Minor Pentatonic scale. By using one hybrid picked legato pattern, we can now cover quite a lot of notes with minimal movement and effort.

Example 7u

Example 7v extends the pattern seen above and adds a bend and vibrato to create a complete, hybrid-picked, Minor Pentatonic lick.

Example 7v

Example 7w is a B Blues Scale lick that I often use in my own playing. By avoiding picking each individual string, I can create longer, smoother lines. This lick uses the second finger, but you can adapt the picking pattern if this seems uncomfortable to you.

Example 7w

Example 7x contains a Blues-Rock double-stop and is reminiscent of guitarists like Stevie Ray Vaughan and Chuck Berry.

Example 7x

As seen in Example 7m it is easy to create intervallic leaps with hybrid picking. This pattern uses the B Natural Minor scale and moves from a low octave up to a high vibrato bend to complete the lick.

Example 7y

Example 7z is the final hybrid picked lick in this book and uses the B Blues Scale to create a modern sound. As with all of the examples in this book, listen to how I play this lick, so that you can copy my articulation and phrasing.

Example 7z

Conclusion

There is a lot of content in this chapter, so return here often in order to keep developing your hybrid picking technique.

Take your time and remember there is no rush to complete a chapter – it is not a race! What matters is that you progress consistently over the next few months and years and that you monitor your development.

Regularly record your practice – either with just audio, or better still, video. Date the recording so you can see and hear just how far you have come. If you play gigs, get a friend to capture recordings for your 'personal development vault'. Be constructive about your playing and always look for positives.

Remember that this book, and your guitar playing, should be about enjoyment, so make having fun your priority, and any challenges will feel less significant by comparison.

Chapter Eight – Dynamics

Dynamics are one of the most overlooked elements of guitar playing. As guitarists, we tend to spend more time thinking about the melodic options available to us, rather than to *how* a note is played. The ability to play a note at any volume or intensity can draw a listener in or blow them away! Dynamics can also emphasize a specific note or phrase or punctuate your licks to make your guitar playing sound expressive and well constructed.

To vary dynamics you must control the way the strings are picked. To pick quietly, use a light touch and apply less force than when you wish to play loudly. Also, experiment with less of the pick being in contact with the string. If a note is played with the very tip of the pick, the volume will be much lower. When you wish to play loudly, aim to create a deeper pick-stroke and play harder and more aggressively.

The more comfortable you become at alternating dynamics, the more you will find you can create varied and interesting tones. It can be good to exaggerate your pick strokes at first, to get used to the variations that can be achieved, before reining yourself in to make subtle adjustments to your volume and tone.

I recommend using a medium to thick pick, as it will give you more control than lighter picks. All the examples recorded in this book are played using a Jim Dunlop Jazz 3 pick.

Different dynamics and timbres can give the guitar a vocal quality so listening to vocalists that have outstanding control over their dynamic range is a great place to start. Freddie Mercury (the lead singer of Queen) was a master of varying dynamics and could sing everything from pop (Somebody to Love), to rock (Bohemian Rhapsody). Female singers, such as Whitney Houston and Randy Crawford, regularly stunned crowds with their vocal range and control.

As well as listening to excellent vocalists, there are, of course, numerous guitar players whose dynamic control and expression is phenomenal. My favorites include Albert King's raw track, Born Under A Bad Sign, Steve Vai's For the Love of God, and Toto's (Steve Lukather) Rosanna. Other expressive players include Jeff Beck, Brian May, David Gilmour, Eric Clapton and B.B. King. Although this book is about melodic rock guitar soloing, check out musicians from all genres, especially the Blues, when listening for dynamic variation.

Dynamics consist of more than just volume. The *tone* that the note produces also plays a vital part in your sound. Notice the difference between a note that is picked using a plectrum and a note that has been finger-picked. The sound produced by a plastic pick is very different from that of the fingers.

Hammer-ons and legato often produce less volume variation than picking every note individually, but can sound smoother and more flowing. A pull-off or tapped note can sound louder than the note that follows it which creates the potential for wide volume variation.

Achieving a great guitar sound is about how *every* note is played. Notice not only *how* you pick each note, but also the *tone* that each pick produces as this will help to quickly develop your individual sound.

In standard music notation, volume dynamics are often shown using letters. The most common are 'p' (*piano* or 'softly') and 'f', (*forte* or 'loudly'). You will also see the letter 'm' (*mezzo* or 'medium'). The letters 'mp' mean 'play quite quietly and 'mf' 'means play quite loudly' When you next read a piece of music, look for these letters to show you how a bar or phrase should be played.

The simplest way to practice dynamics to use just one note, and in the first example we will gradually get louder (crescendo), and quieter (decrescendo).

Example 8a – (Crescendo and Decrescendo)

Example 8b is the reverse of Example 8a. It starts off by getting quieter in bar one, then gradually louder in bar three. Examples 8a and 8b will help to develop your dynamic definition and range.

Example 8b – (Decrescendo and Crescendo)

The following table shows some ideas to help you practice dynamic picking.

First Play:	Then Play:
4 Notes Loudly	4 Notes Quietly
4 Notes Quietly	4 Notes Loudly
2 Notes Loudly	2 Notes Quietly
2 Notes Quietly	2 Notes Loudly
1 Note Loudly	1 Note Quietly
1 Note Quietly	1 Note Loudly
3 Notes Loudly	3 Notes Quietly
3 Notes Quietly	3 Notes Loudly
5 Notes Loudly	5 Notes Quietly
5 Notes Quietly	5 Notes Loudly

Example 8c introduces a C Blues Scale (C Eb F Gb G Bb) pattern. Although on paper it looks easy, applying the dynamic variations chart shown above can be tricky. Set a metronome to 60bpm and play the phrase with each note at an even volume. Next, work through each dynamic variation in the chart above. Accentuate the pick strokes to create the maximum difference between loud and soft, and don't worry about making it sound musical for now; this exercise is all about building your dynamic technique.

The odd note-groupings of one, three and five will feel far trickier than the even-note groupings, so spend extra time on the variations that feel difficult to play and don't move onto Example 8d until the whole chart has been completed.

Example 8c

Example 8d contains some 'mini arpeggios' in the key of Cm. Once again use the dynamic variations chart above and play this example with each variation.

Example 8d

The following Cm Blues Scale lick introduces the challenge of adding dynamic picking to bends. This is will make your lead guitar solos much more emotive. Once again, start off at 60bpm and slowly build the tempo up to around 100bpm.

Example 8e

Progress tracker

It doesn't matter how long it takes you to develop the examples in this chapter, what is important is that they are accurate. Remember the golden guitar adage 'Speed is a by-product of accuracy'. Use the chart below to monitor your progress.

Example	60bpm	70bpm	80bpm	90bpm	100bpm
9a					
9b					
9c					
9d					
9e					

Vocal Dynamics

One way to develop dynamic variation is to copy the dynamics of vocal melodies and play them in different octaves on the guitar. An additional benefit of this is that transcribing melody by ear and listening carefully to the nuance of each phrase helps you develop quickly as a musician and naturally incorporate new ideas.

Really focus on how each note is formed, how loudly, or quietly is each note is sung, and whereabouts in each phrase the dynamics change. The more carefully you listen, the more you will gain from this technique.

Chapter Nine – Building A Melodic Solo

Backing Track Three

This chapter shows you how to build your own solos from short fragments of melody. All the examples in this section are built over the following chord progression.

Example 9a – (Melodic Rock chord progression)

For a rockier variation on Example 9a, the power chords shown below could be used. They will work better if you want to play the chords with distortion.

Example 9b – (Power chord progression)

Example 9c demonstrates the C Major scale in the 5th position (G shape in the CAGED system). This scale shape is used to create the melodies in this chapter.

Example 9c – (C Major scale in 5th position)

The notes C Major scale can be played in different locations on the neck, (shown below). As you get familiar with the examples in this chapter, try creating your own melodies in new areas of the fretboard.

C Major Scale

The first example will act as the main motif in all of the following exercises. The secret of forming a memorable melody is to create something that the listener can sing easily. When developing melodies on the guitar, try playing them to a friend to see if they can repeat back what you have played. This technique was famously used at the Abbey Road studios where songwriters would test out melodies on the public to see their reactions.

Example 9d – (Main melody)

To make the melody in Example 9d more expressive we can add different playing techniques to articulate the phrase. In the next example I have added some slides.

Example 9e – (Main melody with slides)

Next, the original melodic motif is adapted to include some bends. You can experiment with your own articulations as long as the main melody retains the same notes and rhythm.

Example 9f – (Main melody with bends)

Hammer-ons and pull-offs help to provide a smooth, free-flowing legato approach to soloing, and they are added here to enhance the main melody.

Example 9g – (Main melody with legato)

Vibrato is one of the most expressive techniques that the guitar can produce. By adding gentle, vocal-style vibrato to certain notes, the melody can be transformed from a simple pattern into a melodic phrase.

Example 9h – (Main melody with vibrato)

In the previous examples, we added one technique at a time to a melody to create the beginnings of a new solo. It is normal to use many phrasing techniques within each phrase, so the following example shows the same melody with a variety of added articulations.

Example 9i – (Main melody with multiple articulations)

The unique thing about the guitar is that one phrase can be played in many different locations on the fretboard. The following examples explore the melody in various octaves on the guitar. The higher pitched examples shown here are usually more appropriate in a solo, but it's worth experimenting with every placement of the melody over Backing Track Three.

Example 9j – (Main motif in low octave)

In Example 9j, the original melodic line was moved to a lower octave on the guitar. Example 9k uses that same octave but introduces hammer-ons, pull-offs, slides, and vibrato to make the melody more expressive.

Example 9k – (Low octave with articulations)

In the next position, use the same motif higher up on the fretboard in a different octave. Artists like Joe Satriani often create melodic instrumental pieces that play the same melody in different octaves to lift the tune. A tremendous example of this technique is the song Cryin'.

Example 9l – (Main motif in high octave)

Once again, apply expressive techniques to the higher pitched melody. You will find that certain positions on the guitar fit some guitar techniques better than others. Example 9m works well with bends. However, Example 9k doesn't suit bending as well.

Example 9m – (High octave with articulations)

Now that we are familiar with this melody in a variety of areas on the fretboard, we will connect up two different positions using a linking phrase derived from the C Major scale. Example 9n uses slides to move fluidly up the neck allowing us access to different forms of the original melodic motif.

Example 9n – (Linking octaves)

Example 9o adds legato phrasing to the slides previously used in Example 9n. Refer to the full neck diagram to see where these notes come from.

Example 9o – (Linking octaves)

The following example uses bends and slides to move up the neck. The bends create a Blues-Rock sound and work well in any melodic rock solo.

Example 9p – (Linking octaves)

Example 9q uses three-note legato phrases on the B string. Use your first, second and fourth fingers to play each shape.

Example 9q – (Linking octaves)

Now that we can play the motif in multiple octaves and have learnt some linking ideas, we can start to put them together into longer ideas. Example 9r uses the motif in two different octaves and connects them using Example 9p. I love building longer melodies and lines from a simple phrase played in different octaves with a few short linking ideas.

There are two ways to create this type of solo: Start with a chord progression and write a melody to fit over the top of it, or write a melody and fit a chord progression around it later.

Begin with a scale you are familiar with and create a short melody. Loop this melody until you are happy with it and then begin to add expressive techniques such as bends, vibrato, hammer-ons, pull-offs and slides. Once a melody is created with these techniques, move the phrases into different octaves on the guitar. Finally, create some licks that link between each different octave as fluidly as possible.

This approach is a terrific way to ensure your solos are always melodic and memorable!

Example 9r – (Mini solo using examples 10i, 10m and 10p)

Chapter Ten – Single String Improvisation

Backing Track Four

I am often asked, "How did you learn to improvise?" In my early days of playing guitar I didn't have a teacher, but I did have a reasonably good ear. I would pick up every CD in the house and try to solo over as many tracks in as many different genres as possible. At first, everything sounded the same and often quite dull, but after a while, I started to be able to play my guitar confidently and rely on my ear as a guide: An approach I still use to this day!

As I progressed, I began to learn structured approaches to improvisation and I will share my favourites, in the following chapters. Remember that very little of what you hear played on songs is truly improvised. The majority is pre-prepared licks and lines that are played in slightly different ways.

One common problem faced when improvising is the seemingly endless number of scale and position possibilities available to us. By limiting our solos to just one string, we reduce the options available and force ourselves to make the most of each and every note we play.

This chapter will show how scales can be played on a single string, and also how to construct and write licks using a single-string approach. Once a lick has been built on a single string, I will show you how to translate that lick onto different parts of the fretboard.

The examples in this chapter will be played over the following chord progression.

Chord Progression – (Backing Track Four)

We will examine how to play three different scales over the chord progression above. The three scales are C# Minor Pentatonic (C# E F# G# B), C# Blues (C# E F G G# B) and C# Natural Minor (C# D# E F# G# A B).

The first example shows the C# Minor Pentatonic scale played along the B string. Alternate pick each note and get used its shape played on a single string.

Example 10a

C# Minor Pentatonic

An excellent way to practice everything in this chapter is to practice with your eyes closed. This way you will know you have got the ideas under your fingers and are not using your eyes as a guide.

Example 10b brings the above C# Minor Pentatonic shape to life with bends, vibrato and slides.

Example 10b

Although this lick sounds great, there are definitely easier ways to play it. Example 10c is the same phrase, but this time, played across multiple strings for ease.

By writing a lick on a single string you can focus on the sound of the melodic line you are creating and not get side-tracked by the availability of other notes in the position. After writing a lick on a single string, transfer the same notes onto multiple strings for convenience.

Example 10c

The next example shows the same phrase as the previous two ideas, but is now played in another part of the neck, showing that a single-string lick can be moved to many different positions.

Example 10d

By learning one lick in multiple parts of the neck, you maximise the value gained from a single idea. Even though the notes being played are the same, the effect will vary depending on where you play them on the neck. Try playing Example 10c then Example 10d and hear how they differ in tone. Example 10c has a more 'trebley' tonality while 10d produces a warmer sound.

For your reference, here is the C# Minor Pentatonic scale mapped out over the neck. Learn the scale on another single string and practice it over Backing Track Four.

Now that you have learnt the C# Minor Pentatonic Scale on a single string and created a melodic lick, move on to using the C# Blues Scale, to add a different feel to the soloing idea.

Example 10e shows the C# Blues Scale on the B string. Once again, after you have memorised it, learn to play with your eyes closed.

Example 10e

When you have learnt the C# Blues Scale on the B string it is time to create a lick. Example 10f combines slides, bends and vibrato to create a modern sounding rock lick.

Example 10f

Now move this single-string C# Blues lick onto multiple strings to make it easier to play.

Example 10g

This lick can be played in the following location:

Example 10h

Here is the complete C# Blues Scale neck diagram. Experiment by using a different string to make melodies.

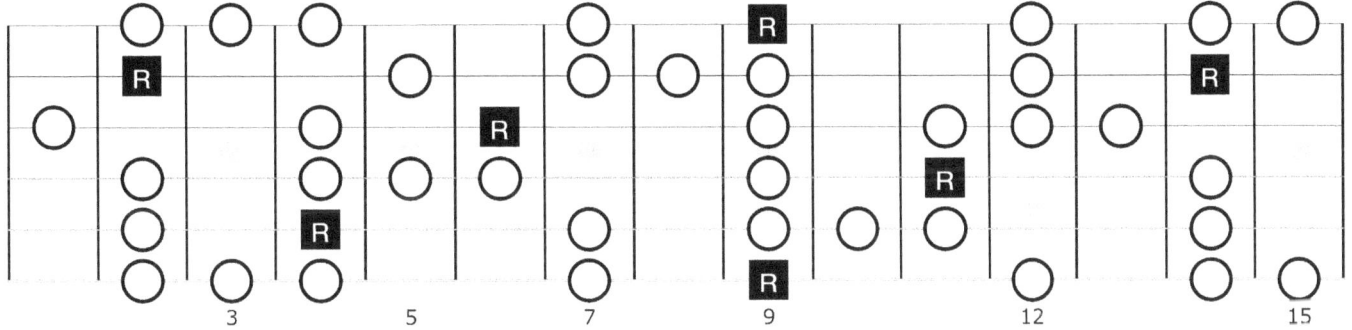

By now, you should be getting the idea of how you can create a melodic phrase. Start with a one-string scale, write a lick using just that single string, then rearrange your lick across multiple strings for convenience and ease.

Example 10i shows the C# Natural Minor scale on the B string.

Example 10i

C# Natural Minor

Now it's time to create a single-string C# minor lick that will work well over Backing Track Four. This four-bar lick works well over the chord progression at the beginning of this chapter.

Example 10j

Move that single string lick onto multiple strings so that you can fret it easily. It is also good practice to learn to play it in different keys.

Example 10k

Example 10l uses a different part of the neck to fret the notes in the previous lick. The guitar is so versatile you can play a lick in any number of positions to create subtly different phrasing.

Example 10l

I have included a few different locations to play each of the previous phrases on the neck although there are other ways you can play them. Try working out your favourite licks from this chapter in as many different locations on the neck as possible.

Here is the full C# Natural Minor scale diagram so you can write single-string licks over Backing Track Four.

C# Natural Minor

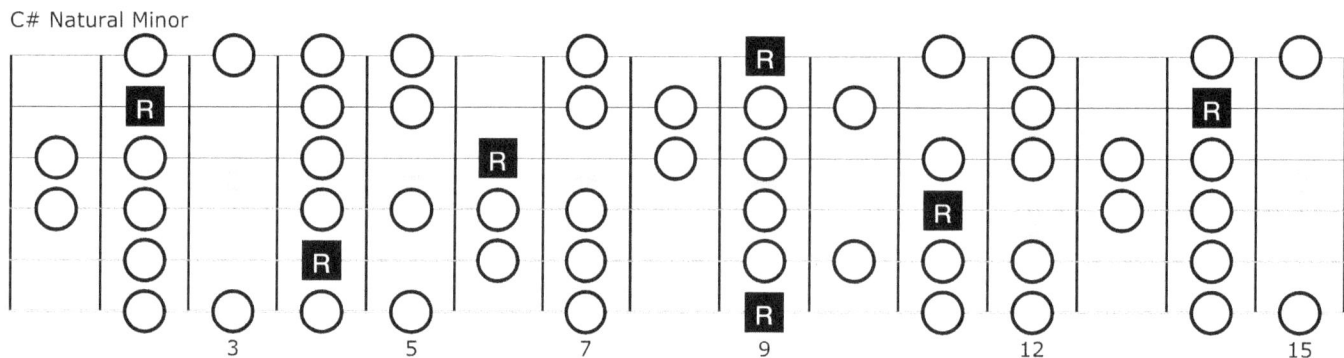

Single string improvisation is my favourite creative soloing strategy in almost any genre of music. It forces me to be aware of exactly what note choices I am making and helps me to break out of the box-shaped scale ruts than can easily occur.

Here is my method for creating useful licks using single strings as the starting point:

1. Find and learn an appropriate scale on a single string (one that fits the track you are playing over).

2. Memorise the scale fully so you can play the scale even with your eyes closed.

3. Create a lick using the scale. It can use any combination of notes, and any technique you wish. Be as creative as you can.

4. Play the new lick over the track you are working on and ensure that it works well.

5. Move the notes of your single-string lick into different parts of the guitar, so wherever you end up in your solo you can have access to your newly written lick.

Chapter Eleven – Double-stop Improvisation

Backing Track Four

Continuing on from the single string techniques we learnt in the previous chapter, we will now look at another of my favourite improvisation strategies.

Most of the time when we improvise on the guitar, we use single-note phrases to create licks. A common way to add variety to solos is to play two-note *double-stops*. To hear double-stops in action, listen to the solo from the Wind Cries Mary by Jimi Hendrix, which is a wonderful demonstration of both double-stops and single note Blues-Rock ideas.

We will use the same C# minor scales and backing track as in the last chapter to provide a sense of continuity while we explore adjacent, and non-adjacent string double-stops. The vast double-stop options available are a fun way to spice up your playing.

The Minor Pentatonic scale

The following example shows the scale of C# Minor Pentatonic scale on just the B and E strings. Learn each pair of notes as double-stop shapes, and play them with your eyes closed as soon as you have committed them to memory.

Example 11a

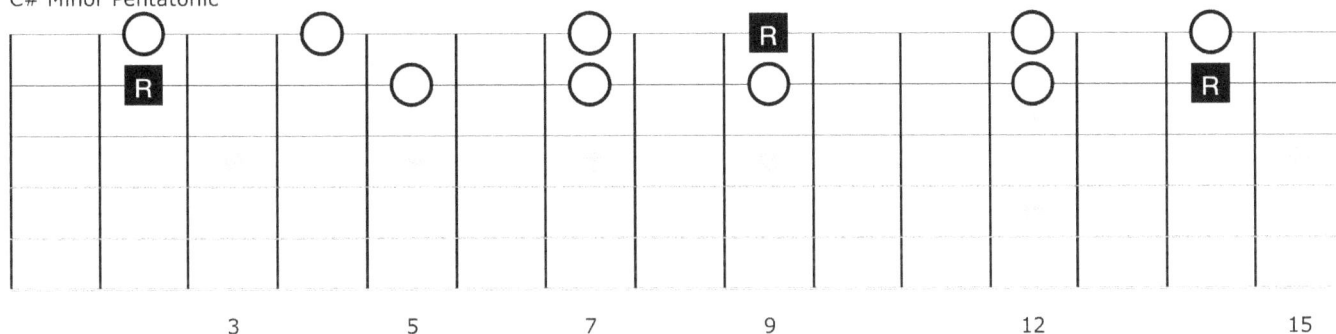

Once you have learnt these double-stop patterns it is time to write a lick with them. The first approach we will look at is to use slides as they are an effective way to move between each position.

Example 11b

The next idea combines the shapes learnt in Example 11a with single-note. Bar four is reminiscent of Hendrix's playing, especially in his solo in The Wind Cries Mary.

Example 11c

The following example shows the C# Minor Pentatonic scale on just the G and B strings. Slowly learn the double-stop pairs with a metronome set to 80bpm. You can play all the ideas in this chapter with Backing Track Four.

Example 11d

C# Minor Pentatonic

Example 11e explores a sliding pattern between the double-stops. Although simple, this approach can form the basis of many longer double-stop licks in your own solos.

Example 11e

The next idea shows that by adding a rhythmic pattern, double-stops can become a useful soloing tool. Watch out for the Hendrix-style hammer-ons at the end of bar four.

Example 11f

Now the fun really starts! Here we have the C# Minor Pentatonic scale on non-adjacent strings (the G and high E strings). These wider intervals are popular in rock, pop and country soloing, and may sound familiar to you.

Example 11g

C# Minor Pentatonic

Once again, by adding slides we can create a useful two-bar phrase. This next lick is almost identical in bars one and two, with just a slight alteration to the final double-stop.

Example 11h

Example 11i is an extension of the previous idea. Remember that the double-stops shown in this pattern are only a starting point for you to investigate. Your ears decide what sounds best, so always let them have the final say!

Example 11i

The final approach to the C# Minor Pentatonic scale is on the D and B strings. Don't worry if these shapes are a little harder to memorise. The more you play and use them in your solos the easier they will become.

Example 11j

C# Minor Pentatonic

Example 11k is a four-bar pattern to fit over Backing Track Four that uses the double-stop shapes from the previous example. This lick will help you see some of the less obvious two-note patterns that can be created. Remember, you can mix and match patterns as you see fit, and the options shown in this chapter are just a starting point for you to explore your own creativity.

Example 11k

The Blues Scale

The C# Blues Scale forms the basis of the next few ideas, and Example 11l shows it on just the top two strings. Remember, we are exploring two-note shapes in this chapter, so view the diagram in terms of double-stops and not single note patterns.

Some of the double-stop shapes shown below are easier on the ear than others. The shapes that have more dissonance to them act as *passing notes* between other double-stops. Experiment with the shapes and licks in this section to get used to playing the Blues scale double-stop.

Example 11l

Example 11m introduces quarter-tone bends and slides to create a musical double-stop lick on the highest strings.

Example 11m

In the next example, the C# Blues scale is played as double-stops on the G and the B strings. Although the ideas in this chapter are all in C#, transpose them to other keys to explore different key-centres.

Example 11n

C# Blues

Let's create a lick using the patterns from the previous example. Example 11o uses an off-beat rhythmic idea and introduce a quarter-tone bend and slide to complete the phrase.

Example 11o

The following ideas look at some non-adjacent string patterns using the C# Blues Scale. Here are the shapes to use on the G and high E strings.

Example 11p

This four-bar pattern has a melodic, tasteful sound, and fits perfectly over Backing Track Four. It combines a mixture of rhythms with slides and a pull-off legato run to create a smooth, fluid feel. The fingering here can be a little tricky so take some time to explore what works best for you.

Example 11q

Now we move onto the D and B string shapes for the C# Blues Scale.

Example 11r

C# Blues

Next, we use hammer-ons and slides to move effortlessly between the two-note shapes. Listen closely to the audio recording to hear how I phrase this example.

Example 11s

The Natural Minor scale

We will now explore the adjacent and non-adjacent string double-stops in C# Natural Minor. Example 11t shows the C# Natural Minor Scale on the high B and E strings.

Example 11t

I don't normally recommend 'noodling' or fiddling about with a scale shape. However, after you have committed all these double-stop shapes to memory, some constructive 'noodling' will be useful. Play along with a metronome, drum track or Backing Track Four and try to create melodies or musical ideas.

Remember that when you are practicing new things, they are unlikely to sound incredible at first. In time, dedicated practice of double-stops will mean that they can be included wherever you like in your playing.

Example 11u uses the C# Natural Minor scale on the high 'E' and 'B' strings exclusively. By incorporating slides and hammer-ons, we can create a Hendrix-style four-bar phrase.

Example 11u

Here are the G and B string double-stop shapes of C# Natural Minor.

Example 11v

Example 11w is somewhere between a lead lick and a rhythm playing idea. It shows a 1/16th note pattern that uses double-stops over the chord progression in Backing Track Four.

Example 11w

Now we move onto the G and high E string shapes of C# Natural Minor. I love this sound and it is often a feature of my rock guitar solos.

Example 11x

In Example 11y, we apply a simple sliding pattern to the shapes from the previous example. Remember that the licks here are just a starting point for your own ideas.

Example 11y

In Example 11z, we explore the D and B string shapes of C# Natural Minor. Notice how some notes remain static as the upper or lower notes move.

Example 11z

C# Natural Minor

Example 11za is the final example in this chapter. It includes hammer-ons and slides to make the double-stops into a melodic rock phrase.

Example 11za

Double-stops Conclusion

Double-stops sound superb in both rhythm and lead guitar playing. By breaking away from playing single note lead licks, you will find that you can create much more variety in your solos. For instance, you could construct solos in the following ways:

1. Single notes only.

2. Double-stops adjacent strings only.

3. Double-stops non-adjacent strings only.

4. All double-stops.

5. Single notes and double-stops adjacent strings only.

6. Single notes and double-stops non-adjacent strings only.

7. Single notes and all adjacent string double-stops and non-adjacent string double-stops.

By combining single notes and double-stops, you now have seven different approaches to soloing. If you're getting a bored with your playing and want to try some new approaches, refer to these ideas.

Put on a backing track and work your way through each of the options shown above. Begin by using just one concept (for example 'single notes only') and when you are happy with that, move on to the next idea. When all seven have been completed separately, combine them in any way you wish.

Chapter Twelve – Full Solo

Backing Track Five

There is nothing quite like learning a guitar solo in its entirety to help you internalise and master new techniques. While learning licks and techniques are a solid base for progression on the guitar, they won't ever provide the satisfaction that you get from playing along, note-for-note with a piece of music.

The following study solo combines all the techniques and ideas seen throughout this book into a fun, melodic solo. The solo is in the key of B minor and uses the B Blues Scale (B D E F F#A) and the B Natural Minor (B C# D E F# G A) scales.

The chord progression throughout is a fairly common pop sequence and the chords are shown below. I recommend that you strum and play the chord progression before learning the solo to feel how the harmony affects the melody.

A breakdown of the solo follows the full transcription, and the scale patterns used are as follows:

B Blues

B Natural Minor

Chords that back the solo

Example 12a: – (B Minor Melodic Rock Solo)

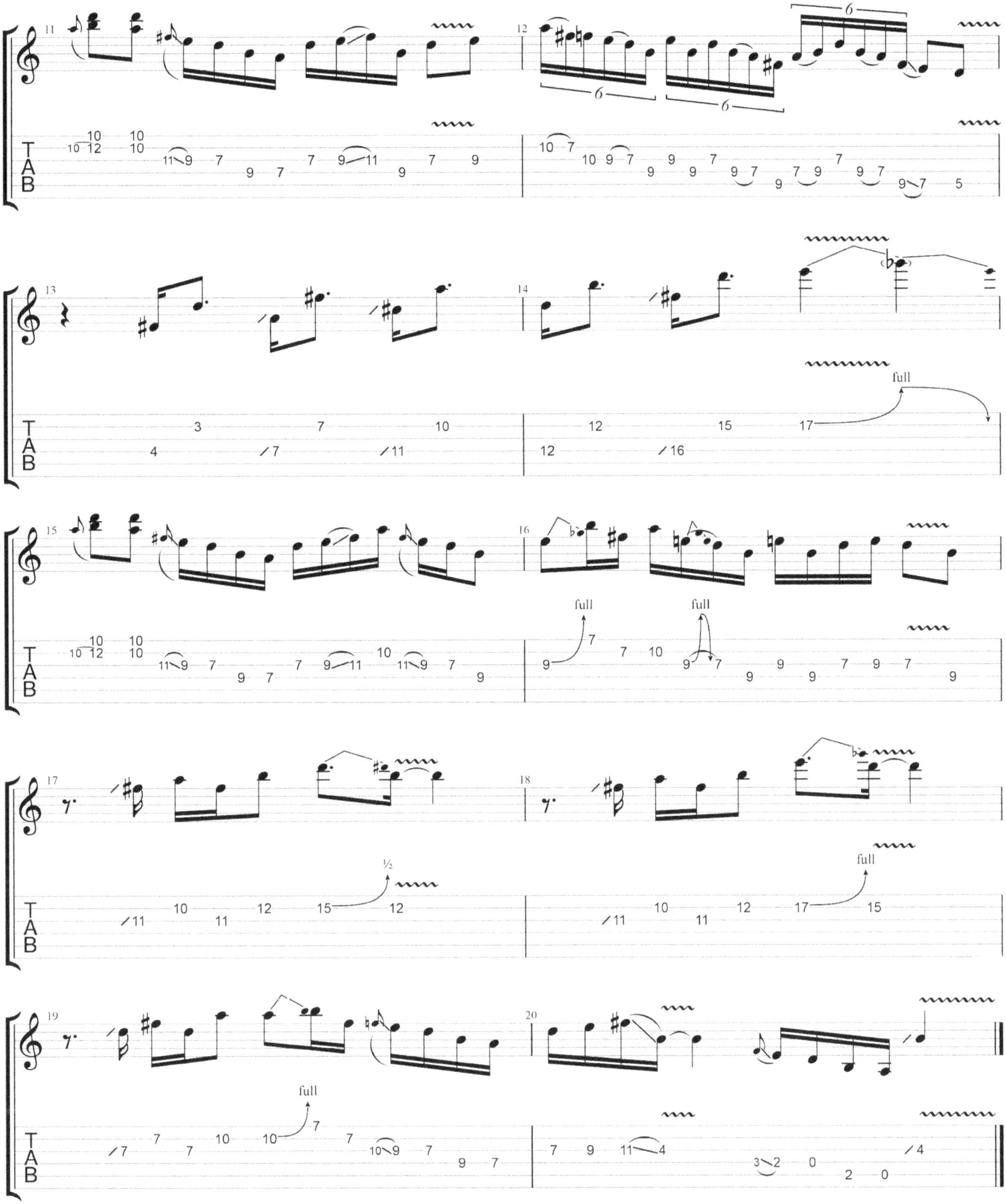
full
½
TAB

Before attempting to play this solo, listen to the audio track at least three times before using the slow version to help you copy each bar individually. This way you will capture every nuance and master the correct phrasing.

Bars 1-4 introduce the call and response theme seen throughout. The call is a simple bending idea, and the response is a B Blues lick with slides and a quarter-tone bend. Bar three repeats the lick from bar one and bar four uses a longer B Blues double-stop idea.

Bars 4-8 repeats the call and response theme introduced in bars one to four but an octave higher. This is a great way to maximise a theme and create a longer solo piece.

Bars 7-12 introduce some longer, B Natural Minor runs and it will require practice to nail each note. As always, listen first, then copy each phrase with a metronome set to about 70bpm.

Bar 13 includes some of the non-adjacent string double-stops we studied in Chapter Eleven. These break up the single note lines wonderfully and add colour to the melodic construction of the solo.

Bars 14-end rounds up the solo with different shapes of the B Blues and B Natural Minor scales. I applied rhythmic variations and many different techniques to create this section.

This solo was created by recording my improvisation over the backing track before extracting my favourite licks from various takes into one 'constructed' solo. This is a good way for you to create strong, memorable solos. Begin by recording your improvisations and listen back to find your favourite parts, and then simply put them together into a super solo!

Chapter Thirteen – Famous Rock Tones

Now that you have mastered these techniques and improvisational strategies, it is time to talk about how your guitar tone effects melodic rock soloing. In the following section, I reference three outstanding melodic-rock guitarists and talk about how they create their individual sounds. Listen to each song reference as you read about their tone.

Pink Floyd (David Gilmour) – Another Brick in The Wall

David Gilmour is one of the most skilful Blues-Rock guitarists ever to pick up the instrument. As well as developing his own unique bending techniques (like the two tone bend seen earlier), his phrasing is as smooth as silk and Gilmour has one of the purest tones around.

Gilmour is famous for his black Fender Stratocaster, and most of the early Pink Floyd records were recorded using this guitar. He had a custom pickup designed, which later went into production as the SSL-5. He uses a custom string gauge of 0.10, 0.12, 0.16, 0.28, 0.38 and 0.48 which are available from GHS Boomers.

Toto (Steve Lukather) – Rosanna

Steve Lukather has played his signature Luke guitar made by Ernie Ball for many years and has been famous for his thick, heavy-rock sound since the 1980s.

He now uses Bogner amplifiers and favours the Ecstasy 101b head through a Bogner 4x12 cabinet. Lukather runs many delay and reverb effects pedals, including the Strymon Blue Sky Reverberator, TC Electronic Flashback, and the Hardwire DL-8. His modulation effects pedals include the BenRod Electro Wave Box, Strymon Lex Rotary and the Providence Anadime chorus. He also favours the Jim Dunlop Joe Bonamassa signature Cry Baby Wah pedal.

Carlos Santana – Smooth

Santana is a long-term endorser of PRS guitars. His Latin rock songs are complemented by a warm, rich tone. He has used Mesa Boogie, Dumble Overdrive Reverb and Bludotone Universal Tone Head amps which create the sound he needs. Santana uses a minimal pedalboard that often features a Pete Cornish line driver and a Real McCoy Custom RMC4 Wah. Santana is living proof that armed with a great guitar and amplifier you don't always need hundreds of pedals!

Although there is no specific set-up that defines a melodic rock guitar sound, there are some fundamental principles that will help you craft the best possible tone.

Get your guitar and amp set up by a professional.

Use fresh strings before recording or playing live (I often like to have played them for a day beforehand, so they are slightly worn in).

Experiment with pick sizes and gauges to see what suits your style.

Buy the best quality cables you can afford.

Only add pedals and effects to your guitar chain once you know your amp inside out. Spend time tweaking all the settings on your amp – volume, gain and EQ – and craft your individual tone with your amp.

Invest in good quality drive, reverb and delay pedals. These form the basis of most melodic rock tones.

Conclusion

Whether you are just beginning your journey, or you are an experienced soloist, everyone's playing will benefit by making melody their priority. Use the examples in this book as a starting point for creating musical lines, phrases and complete songs. Try to let your ears guide you, and don't rely on the finger patterns and scale shapes that you know to be the 'safe' notes. Remember the saying, "If it sounds good, it is. If it sounds bad … it probably is too!"

Practice what you don't know, not what you do! This is quite simply the best advice I can give any musician. Use a metronome to help you master each example and use backing tracks to create a more musical approach to practicing.

An important musical goal should be to play with other people, so while you are developing your skills in this book, find time to jam with other musicians. Playing with other instrumentalists is the best way to improve your musicianship.

If you want to apply melodic rock soloing ideas to different pentatonic scales, then check out my book **Exotic Pentatonic Soloing For Guitar**, which is also available through **www.fundamental-changes.com**

My passion in life is teaching people to play and express themselves through the guitar. If you have any questions, please get in touch and I will do my best to respond as quickly as possible.

You can contact me on **simeypratt@gmail.com** or via the **Fundamental Changes YouTube channel**.

Discography

Pink Floyd - The Wall / Dark Side Of The Moon

Toto - Toto IV

Guns N' Roses – Appetite For Destruction

Gary Moore – Still Got The Blues

Carlos Santana - Amigos

Queen – Day At The Races

Journey - Escape

Eric Johnson – Ah Via Musicom

Jimi Hendrix – Are You Experienced?

Cream – Goodbye Cream

Led Zeppelin – IV

Van Halen – Van Halen

Joe Satriani – The Extremist

Steve Vai – Passion and Warfare

Other Books from Fundamental Changes

The Complete Guide to Playing Blues Guitar Book One: Rhythm Guitar

The Complete Guide to Playing Blues Guitar Book Two: Melodic Phrasing

The Complete Guide to Playing Blues Guitar Book Three: Beyond Pentatonics

The Complete Guide to Playing Blues Guitar Compilation

The CAGED System and 100 Licks for Blues Guitar

Fundamental Changes in Jazz Guitar: The Major ii V I

Minor ii V Mastery for Jazz Guitar

Jazz Blues Soloing for Guitar

Guitar Scales in Context

Guitar Chords in Context Part One

Jazz Guitar Chord Mastery (Guitar Chords in Context Part Two)

Complete Technique for Modern Guitar

Funk Guitar Mastery

The Complete Technique, Theory and Scales Compilation for Guitar

Sight Reading Mastery for Guitar

Rock Guitar Un-CAGED: The CAGED System and 100 Licks for Rock Guitar

The Practical Guide to Modern Music Theory for Guitarists

Beginner's Guitar Lessons: The Essential Guide

Chord Tone Soloing for Jazz Guitar

Heavy Metal Lead Guitar

Exotic Pentatonic Soloing for Guitar

Heavy Metal Rhythm Guitar

Voice Leading Jazz Guitar

The Complete Jazz Soloing Compilation

The Jazz Guitar Chords Compilation

Fingerstyle Blues Guitar

Facebook: **FundamentalChangesInGuitar**